STARTING POINTS

WATER

Su Swallow

Photography by Chris Fairclough

FRANKLIN WATTS
LONDON · NEW YORK · SYDNEY · TORONTO

© 1990 Franklin Watts

First published in Great Britain in 1990 by
Franklin Watts
96 Leonard Street
London EC2A 4RH

First published in Australia by
Franklin Watts Australia
14 Mars Road
Lane Cove
NSW 2066

First published in the United States by
Franklin Watts Inc.
387 Park Avenue South
New York N.Y. 10016

UK ISBN: 0 7496 0229 5

A CIP Catalogue record for this book is available from the British Library.

Series design: David Bennett
Model making: Stan Johnson
Picture Research: Sarah Ridley
Typesetting: Lineage, Watford
Printed in Belgium

Acknowledgement: 'Water' by Leo Carey reprinted by kind permission of Faber and
Faber Ltd, © Leo Carey 1988.

Additional photographs: B & C Alexander 15bl; Heather Angel 12t, 15cr, 22tr;
Chris Fairclough 6-7, 7tr, 8 (both), 20bl, 22-23, 29, 30; Chris Fairclough Colour
Library (Martyn Cattermole) 6tr, (Jack Coulthard) 7tl, (John Davies) 7bl, (Julia
Waterlow) 13bl; Hutchison Library 9t, 14 (both), 22bl, 23tl, 23cr; Oxford
Scientific (G Bernard) 24br; Planet Earth (Peter David) 16l, (Warren Williams) 16r;
Science Photo Library 21tr, 21cl; Tourism Authority of Thailand 23bl; Barrie Watts
17tl, tc, tr; Hamish Wilson 9c; ZEFA 4-5, 6cl, 7br, 9bl, 13t, 13br, 14-15, 17b, 20t,
21tl, 21br, 28 (all).

CONTENTS

A Watery World

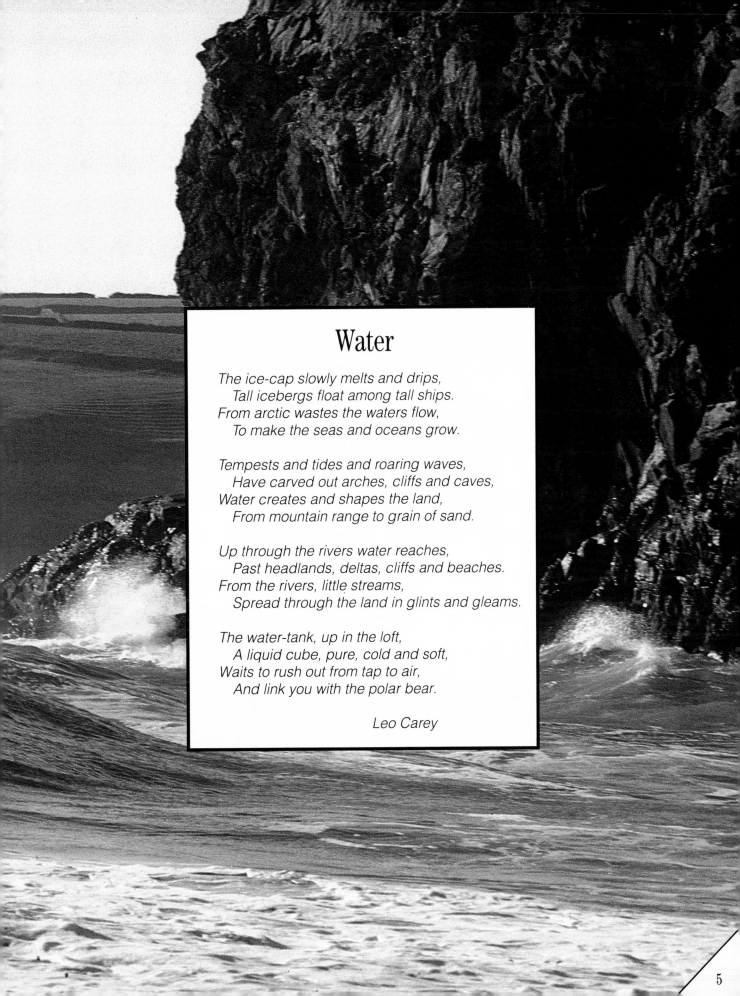

Water

The ice-cap slowly melts and drips,
    Tall icebergs float among tall ships.
From arctic wastes the waters flow,
    To make the seas and oceans grow.

Tempests and tides and roaring waves,
    Have carved out arches, cliffs and caves,
Water creates and shapes the land,
    From mountain range to grain of sand.

Up through the rivers water reaches,
    Past headlands, deltas, cliffs and beaches.
From the rivers, little streams,
    Spread through the land in glints and gleams.

The water-tank, up in the loft,
    A liquid cube, pure, cold and soft,
Waits to rush out from tap to air,
    And link you with the polar bear.

Leo Carey

Water On The Move

Water is always on the move from the sky to the ground and back again. It is called the water cycle.

Some of the rainwater soaks into the ground. The rest flows downhill. The water in mountain streams flows quickly.

Raindrops form round tiny specks of dust in the air. When the drops get too heavy they fall to the ground.

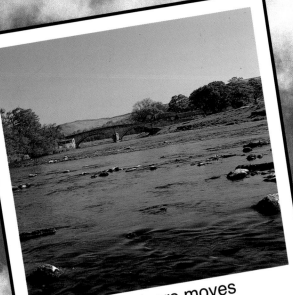

The water in rivers moves slowly because the land is flatter. When a river reaches the coast, the water flows into the sea.

When the Sun warms the sea, some of the water turns into a gas called water vapour. It rises into the air, but it is invisible.

High in the sky the cold air turns the vapour back into drops of water. The drops collect in groups to form clouds.

The tiny drops collide and join together until they are too heavy to stay up in the sky. Then it rains again.

Water On Tap

We live in a part of the world that has plenty of water. When we are thirsty, we just turn on the tap. When we are dirty we can jump in the bath or stand under the shower. We have enough water for cooking and washing. We can use water for fun, too.

There is water almost everywhere on earth: salt water in the seas, fresh water in rivers and lakes and frozen water in the Arctic and Antarctic. But there is very little water in deserts, except underground. People who live in desert places often have to walk a long way from their homes to fetch water. They fill their buckets and pots from a well or a water hole. The water is not very clean, but without water the people would die.

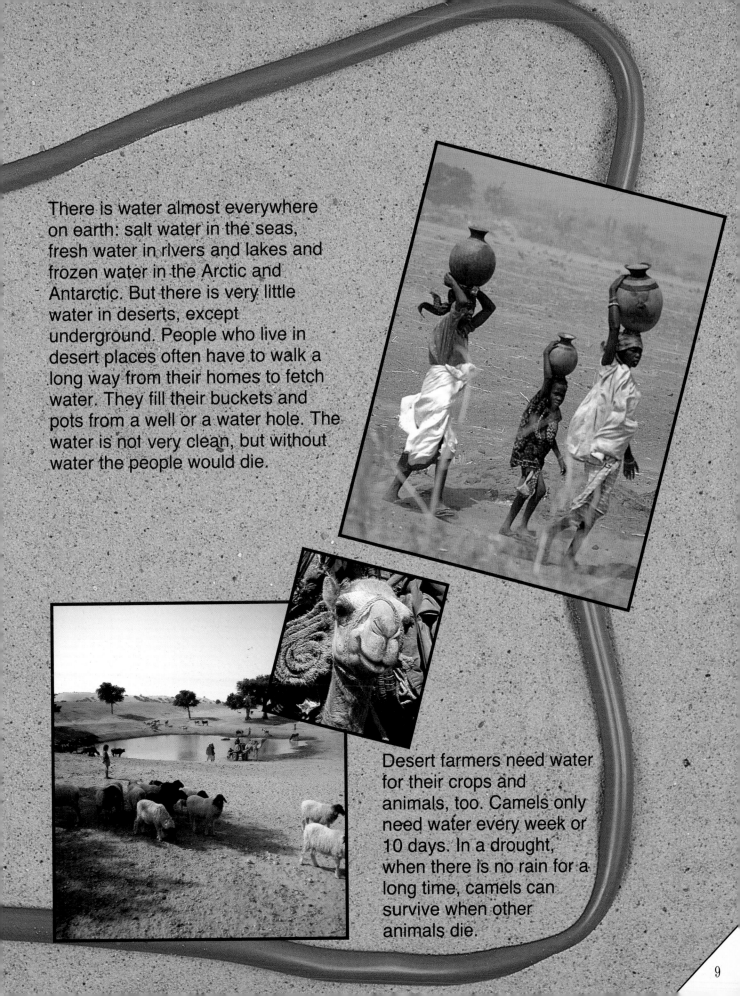

Desert farmers need water for their crops and animals, too. Camels only need water every week or 10 days. In a drought, when there is no rain for a long time, camels can survive when other animals die.

Fruit Drinks

These drinks are easy to make and taste delicious! When you have tried them, you could invent your own recipes.

Lemonade

You will need:

- **2 lemons**
- **30 g white or brown sugar**
- **½ litre water**

What to do:

Wash the lemons and peel them thinly. Put the peel and sugar in a jug (but not a glass one). Boil the water and pour it into the jug. (Ask an adult to help you do this.) Cover and leave the mixture to cool. Squeeze the juice out of the two lemons and add it to the lemonade. Serve very cold.

Fruit Cup

You will need:

- **¼ litre pineapple juice**
- **100 g sugar**
- **Juice of 2 lemons**
- **1 grapefruit, 1 orange, 1 apple**
- **1 banana, a thick slice of pineapple and some grapes**

What to do:

Heat the pineapple juice (ask an adult to help you) and stir in the sugar. Wash the apple and grapes, and peel the rest of the fruit. Cut the fruit into chunks and put them in a bowl. Add the pineapple and lemon juice. Chill the mixture. To serve, put one cup of the fruit mixture into a glass and top up with ice-cold water.

Water For Life

Plants, like people and animals, need water to live.

Desert plants survive for long periods without water. Large cacti store several tonnes of water in their stems. Plants that look dead burst into flower when it rains.

Plants take in water from the soil through tiny hairs on their roots. The water travels up the stem and into the leaves. The leaves use water, sunlight and carbon dioxide from the air to make food. Water that is not needed escapes as vapour through tiny holes on the leaf's surface. As leaves lose water, they replace it with water from the stem, which in turn makes the roots take up more water. The water also keeps the stem and leaves rigid. Without water they droop.

Farmers have to water their crops when it does not rain. Watering crops is called irrigation.

Sometimes water has to be brought up from below ground to irrigate crops. Animals are often used to drive the wheels that lift up the water.

Farmers in Asia flood their fields to grow rice. They dig channels to carry water from a river on to their land. On mountains, they cut terraces to catch water as it flows downhill. Flooded rice fields are called paddy fields.

Water And Weather

Too much rain can be as much of a problem as too little rain.

In parts of India the heavy monsoon rains last for many weeks. These Indians are wearing rain ponchos to keep them dry while they work in the paddy fields. The ponchos are made of woven leaves.

When it rains very hard for a long time, the water may flood the land. The people who lived in this valley in Brazil lost their homes, their crops and their animals.

If all the ice at the North and South Poles melted, the sea would rise by about 65 metres. Many big cities round the world would be flooded.

In the Arctic, some of the ice and snow melt in summer. The water that is left cannot all drain away because the ground below the surface stays frozen.

Life In The Sea

Plants and animals of the sea are specially adapted for life in water.

The angler fish lives in the deepest, darkest parts of the oceans. It uses a luminous growth above its head as a bait to attract its prey. When other fish swim close, the angler fish snaps them up and swallows them whole.

Seaweeds are not like land plants. Instead of roots, most seaweeds cling to rocks with a holdfast. Some have strong stems and leathery fronds which can stand up to the crashing of the waves. Some have air bladders to hold them up.

On the seashore, the tide rises and falls. The creatures who live there are first covered by seawater, then exposed to the air. They have to stay damp at low tide. If they dry out, they die.

Limpets and mussels have watertight shells. Crabs, starfish and other animals hide under rocks or among seaweed. Seaweeds have a coating of slime which keeps them moist until the tide comes in again.

Seawater is salty. The salt can be separated from the water in small areas called pans. The pans are flooded with seawater. When the water evaporates in the Sun, the salt is left behind.

Making Boats

People have travelled across water in all kinds of boats. Make some model boats and see if they float.

A paper boat

1 Fold a sheet of paper 20 cm by 15 cm in half across the middle.

2 Fold up one quarter of the top layer. Fold down the top left and right corners so they touch the middle of the bottom fold.

3 Fold the top point down to touch the bottom fold.

4 Unfold back to stage 1.

5 Turn the paper over. Fold up the bottom quarter of the new top layer. Fold in both corners of this bottom strip.

6 Fold this double strip up once more (ie another quarter). Fold in the corners of the paper underneath. Turn the paper over, keeping all the folds in place.

7 Fold the top corners down again (as in stage 2). Fold up the bottom flap, tucking in the corners at both ends. Fold up again to complete the sides of the boat.

8 Press the boat flat, then pull open from the bottom centre.

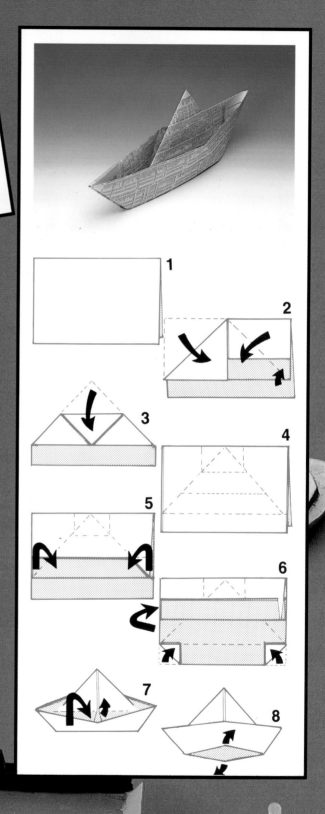

Use a craft knife to cut shapes like these out of balsa wood. (You might need to ask an adult to help you.) Cover the table with a thick layer of newspaper before you begin. Glue the pieces together with wood glue. When the glue is dry, you could paint the boat.

You could make a fleet of ships out of leaves, feathers, walnut shells, wood, cork or paper. Try other materials, too. Try them out in the bath or in a large bowl of water. Which float best? Make sails for some of the boats and blow through a straw to push them along. Which sails work best?

Water Power

Water can be used to power machinery.

In the past, moving water was used to work flour mills. The mills were built beside streams. The water pushed huge paddle wheels round. The wheels drove the machinery that ground the grain into flour.

Today, moving water is used to make electricity. A dam is built across a river to hold the water back. The water pushes hard against the barrier of rock or concrete. When pipes in the dam are opened, the water rushes through. It hits the blades of wheels called turbines. The turbines spin very fast and drive the machines that make electricity.

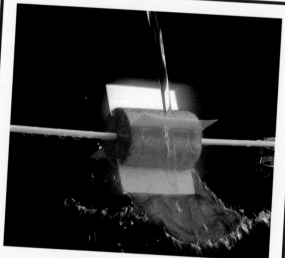

This model shows you how a water turbine works. Ask an adult to make a hole through a large cork. Cut four slots along the cork to hold the blades, cut from an old ice cream tub or from stiff card. Slide the cork on to a knitting needle. Hold the cork under a running tap and watch it spin. What happens if you turn the tap on more?

Surfers use the power of the waves to push them back to the shore on their boards. Wave power can be used to make electricity, too. The crashing waves push air in front of them. The air drives air turbines to generate electricity. Several ways to use wave power are being tested. Here are two of them.

In some parts of the world, hot water bubbles to the earth's surface. The water has been heated by hot rocks under the ground. Steam from the water can be used to drive turbines to make electricity. This power station is in Central America.

Water power could be more important in the future as coal, oil and gas run out.

Water Festivals

Water festivals can be fun, if you don't mind getting wet occasionally!

Ice sculptures form part of the New Year festival in Harbin, in China. Huge blocks of ice are cut from the frozen river and carved into beautiful shapes. Coloured lights are fitted into the sculptures so they light up at night. The sculptures last for several months until they thaw in the spring.

People in Burma spray each other with water as part of their New Year celebrations.

In northern Nigeria, a fishing festival is held at the end of a religious festival called Ramadan, when people fast. Men stand in the river to catch fish in nets. The man who catches the biggest fish wins a prize.

In Thailand in November, people celebrate the end of the rainy season and give thanks to the gods of water. They set lighted candles afloat on rafts of leaves and flowers.

An Aquarium

If you have a pond near you, you can collect some animals and plants and keep them in an aquarium.

Look for different kinds of water snails on water plants. Some may be 5 cm long.

Notice how the animals move and feed. Keep a diary of what happens as tadpoles hatch. (Feed them with tiny pieces of raw fish or meat.) Return the animals and plants to the pond when you have finished studying them.

The larva (young form) of a dragonfly lives in ponds until it is fully grown.

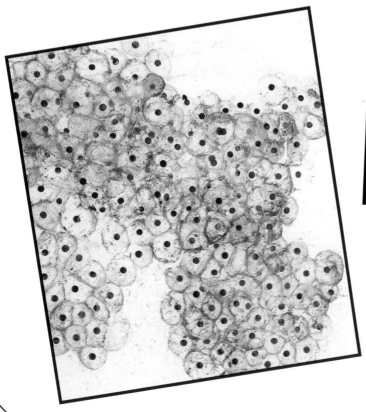

Tadpoles emerge from frogspawn about ten days after the spawn is laid in the water.

The best time to make an aquarium is in spring or summer, when ponds are full of life. Put a layer of clean gravel in the bottom of the tank to anchor the plants. Carefully pour water in. Rain or pond water is best. If you use tap water, leave it for a few days to let the chlorine evaporate. Then stock it.

If you leave your aquarium outside (find somewhere safe), some water creatures will find their own way to it. Indoors, the tank needs a light place away from direct sunlight. Change some of the water from time to time to keep it fresh.

Water Pictures

Paints that mix with water are good for making surprise pictures.

To make a picture like this tiger in the grass, you need:
- **a large sheet of thick paper**
- **powder paints**
- **a straw**

Pour a little blob of paint on to the paper. Now blow the paint across the paper, using the straw. Do the same with other colours. What shapes have you made?

To make a picture like the background on this page or the cockerel opposite, you need:
- **white paper**
- **a white wax candle or wax crayon**
- **some very watery paint**
- **a brush**

Draw all over the paper with the candle or crayon. Then brush paint all over the paper to see what you have drawn.

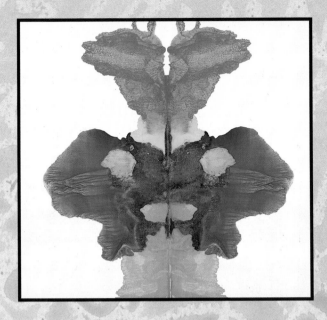

Is it a monster? A man? A butterfly? To make a mystery picture, start by folding a sheet of paper in half. Open out the paper and put blobs of thick paint on the fold line. Fold the sheet again and rub all over with your hand. Open it and see!

Use a piece of kitchen sponge to decorate shapes cut out of white card. Stick the shapes on dark paper to make a big picture.

Clouds

The clouds can give us clues about the weather.

On a stormy day, low cumulus clouds full of water heap up into cauliflower shapes. The top may be white, but the bottom is dark.

The long streaky clouds in the top picture are ice clouds very high in the sky. They are called cirrus clouds. The round fluffy cumulus clouds are lower down and have ice and water in them.

On a fine summer day look for fluffy altocumulus clouds (below). They are a mixture of ice and water.

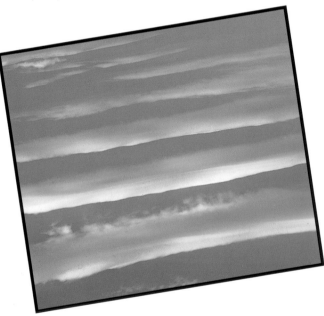

These bands of low stratus clouds have been blown into a stripy pattern by wind blowing over hills or mountains.

Cloud pictures

Collect pictures of cloudy skies from magazines and newspapers. Make a collage.

More Things To Do

Roots and shoots

Some plants can be grown just in water for a time, although they must eventually be planted in soil to grow strong.

Balance an onion in the neck of a jar filled with water. Stick three cocktail sticks round the middle of the onion, if necessary, to rest on the jar rim. The base of the onion should just touch the water. It will soon grow new roots, and shoots may appear, too.

Grow plant cuttings in the same way. Cut leafy stems a few

centimetres long from different plants. Balance them on small jars of water so the base of the stem is in the water. Which plants grow roots?

Water pressure

Dams have to be thicker at the bottom than at the top. This is because the pressure of water is greater the deeper the water is. You can see this for yourself with a simple experiment.

In the sink, fill an old plastic bottle with water. Use a sharp nail to punch a hole in the bottle about half way down. Water will spurt out. Keep the tap running so the bottle stays full. Now make holes above and below the first one. You will see that the bottom jet of water is stronger than the other two. Now turn the tap off and see what happens to the jets of water as the level in the bottle goes down.

Water from nowhere

In an emergency, water can be collected from the ground quite easily. Try this out in the garden to see how it works. Dig a small hole, put a pot in the bottom and cover the hole with a sheet of polythene. Weigh the sheet down with stones, and put one in the middle, above the pot.

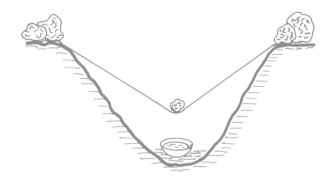

As the Sun warms the earth, water in the soil will escape into the hole as vapour. At night, when the air is cold, the vapour will turn back to water. It will collect on the underside of the sheet and run down into the pot. Dew may collect on the top of the sheet, too.

Water music

Fill several milk bottles with different amounts of water. Tap them with a dowel stick to hear the sound each one makes. Adjust the amount of water in each bottle until you can make a different note with each one. The notes sound lower the more water you put in. The water vibrates and makes the sound.

Try other beaters – perhaps a metal spoon handle or a plastic knitting needle – to change the kind of sound.

If you blow across the bottle, the air in the bottle vibrates and makes the sound. Now the low notes are made by the bottles with more air and less water.

A water quiz

1. In a lake, where is the water pressure greatest?
a) at 5 m
b) at 15 m
c) at 50 m

2. What are cirrus, cumulus and stratus?

3. True or false?
a) In deserts, goats need watering less often than other animals.
b) Raindrops form round tiny specks of dust.
c) Seaweeds have roots.
d) Rice is grown in paddy fields.

4. Which of these is the odd one out?
a) limpet
b) crab
c) dragonfly larva
d) angler fish
e) starfish

5. What is the name of the rainy season in India?
a) water cycle
b) monsoon
c) irrigation

6. Which of these can be used to drive turbines?
a) steam
b) water
c) air

Water words

How would you describe water and watery places? Here are some useful watery words to start you thinking.

Weather words	Moving water
rain	rushing
drizzle	gushing
shower	swirling
cloud	foaming
flood	spray
rainbow	splash
puddle	drip
monsoon	ripple
storm	bubble
Wellington boots	trickle
umbrella	spill
freeze	
thaw	
damp	
misty	
humid	
drenched	
soaking	
soggy	
boggy	
sparkling	
reflections	

Watery places

pond	sea
fountain	whirlpool
stream	marsh
river	oasis
lake	waterfall
canal	

Index

Water quiz answers

1. c) The water pressure is greatest where the water is deepest.

2. Cirrus, cumulus and stratus are kinds of clouds.

3. a) False. Camels need watering less often than other animals.
   b) True.
   c) False. Seaweeds have holdfasts to anchor them to rocks.
   d) True.

4. c) is the odd one out. The dragonfly larva lives in fresh water. All the others live in salt water.

5. b) The rainy season in India is called the monsoon.

6. a), b) and c). Steam ,water and air can all be used to drive turbines.